EASY PORTUGUESE COOKBOOK

50 AUTHENTIC PORTUGUESE AND BRAZILIAN RECIPES

By
Chef Maggie Chow
Copyright © 2015 by Saxonberg
Associates

Published by
BookSumo, a division of Saxonberg
Associates
http://www.booksumo.com/

STAY TO THE END OF THE COOKBOOK AND RECEIVE....

I really appreciate when people, take the time to read all of my recipes.

So, as a gift for reading this entire cookbook you will receive a **massive collection of special recipes.**

Read to the end of and get my *Easy Specialty Cookbook Box Set for FREE*!

This box set includes the following:

1. *Easy Sushi C*
2. *Easy Dump l*
   Cookbook
3. *Easy Beans Cookbook*

Remember this box set is about **EASY** cooking.

In the ***Easy Sushi Cookbook*** you will learn the easiest methods to prepare almost every type of Japanese Sushi i.e. *California Rolls, the Perfect Sushi Rice, Crab Rolls, Osaka Style Sushi*, and so many others.

Then we go on to *Dump Dinners*. Nothing can be easier than a Dump Dinner. In the ***Easy Dump Dinner Cookbook*** we will learn how to master our slow cookers and make some amazingly unique dinners that will take almost ***no effort***.

Finally in the ***Easy Beans Cookbook*** we tackle one of my favorite side dishes: Beans. There are so many delicious ways to make Baked Beans and Bean Salads that I had to share them.

So stay till the end and then keep on cooking with my *Easy Specialty Cookbook Box Set*!

ABOUT THE AUTHOR.

Maggie Chow is the author and creator of your favorite *Easy Cookbooks* and *The Effortless Chef Series*. Maggie is a lover of all things related to food. Maggie loves nothing more than finding new recipes, trying them out, and then making them her own, by adding or removing ingredients, tweaking cooking times, and anything to make the recipe not only taste better, but be easier to cook!

For a complete listing of all my books please see my author page.

INTRODUCTION

Welcome to *The Effortless Chef Series*!
Thank you for taking the time to
download the *Easy Portuguese
Cookbook*. Come take a journey with me
into the delights of easy cooking. The
point of this cookbook and all my
cookbooks is to exemplify the effortless
nature of cooking simply.

In this book we focus on Portuguese and
Brazilian cooking. You will find that
even though the recipes are simple, the
taste of the dishes is quite amazing.

So will you join me in an adventure of
simple cooking? If the answer is yes
(and I hope it is) please consult the table
of contents to find the dishes you are
most interested in. Once you are ready
jump right in and start cooking.

— Chef Maggie Chow

TABLE OF CONTENTS

ANY ISSUES? CONTACT ME

If you find that something important to you is missing from this book please contact me at maggie@booksumo.com.

I will try my best to re-publish a revised copy taking your feedback into consideration and let you know when the book has been revised with you in mind.

:)

— Chef Maggie Chow

LEGAL NOTES

COMMON ABBREVIATIONS

cup(s)	C.
tablespoon	tbsp
teaspoon	tsp
ounce	oz.
pound	lb

*All units used are standard American measurements

CHAPTER 1: EASY PORTUGUESE AND BRAZILIAN RECIPES

PORTUGUESE BREAD

Ingredients

- 1 C. milk
- 1 egg
- 2 tbsps margarine
- 1/3 C. white sugar
- 3/4 tsp salt
- 3 C. bread flour
- 2 1/2 tsps active dry yeast

Directions

- To make this bread grab your bread maker. Enter the following into it: yeast, milk, flour, beaten eggs, salt, and margarine.

- Set the bread machine to its basic cycle and let the machine go.
- Let the bread sit for 10 mins before serving.
- Enjoy.

Amount per serving (12 total)

Timing Information:

Preparation	5 m
Cooking	3 h
Total Time	3 h 5 m

Nutritional Information:

Calories	179 kcal
Fat	3.2 g
Carbohydrates	31.7g
Protein	5.6 g
Cholesterol	17 mg
Sodium	181 mg

* Percent Daily Values are based on a 2,000 calorie diet.

COD CASSEROLE

Ingredients

- 2 lbs salted cod fish
- 5 large potatoes, peeled and sliced
- 3 large onions, sliced
- 3/4 C. olive oil
- 2 cloves garlic, minced
- 1 tbsp diced fresh parsley
- 1 1/2 tsps crushed red pepper flakes
- 1 tsp paprika
- 3 tbsps tomato sauce

Directions

- Submerge your cod in water for 8 hrs. Then remove all the liquids and let it sit for another 8 hours in new water.
- Now get a saucepan boiling with more fresh water.

- Once the water is boiling place your cod into the pot and cook the fish for 7 mins.
- At the same time set your oven to 375 degrees before doing anything else.
- Get a bowl, combine: tomato sauce, olive oil, paprika, garlic, pepper flakes, and parsley.
- Place your potato pieces into a baking dish and then layer the cod and then the onions over the potato. Now add more potatoes and the dry mix.
- Cook everything for 50 mins in the oven.
- Enjoy.

Amount per serving (12 total)

Timing Information:

Preparation	20 m
Cooking	45 m
Total Time	1 d 1 h 5 m

Nutritional Information:

Calories	476 kcal
Fat	15.6 g
Carbohydrates	31.9g
Protein	50.5 g
Cholesterol	1115 mg
Sodium	5346 mg

* Percent Daily Values are based on a 2,000 calorie diet.

PASTEIS DE NATA

(PORTUGUESE CUSTARD DESSERT)

Ingredients

- 1 C. milk
- 3 tbsps cornstarch
- 1/2 vanilla bean
- 1 C. white sugar
- 6 egg yolks
- 1 (17.5 oz.) package frozen puff pastry, thawed

Directions

- Coat a muffin pan with nonstick spray or oil and set your oven to 375 degrees before doing anything else.
- Heat the following, while mixing, until it is thick: vanilla, milk, sugar, and cornstarch.

- Now get a bowl, add in your yolks and half of a C. of the vanilla mix.
- Stir the mix until it is smooth, and add the yolks into the pot and stir the contents again.
- Stir and cook this mix for 6 more mins and then discard the beans.
- Now line the sides and bottom of the muffin tin with puff pastry and top the pastry with the vanilla mix.
- Cook everything for 25 mins in the oven.
- Enjoy.

Amount per serving (12 total)

Timing Information:

Preparation	20 m
Cooking	20 m
Total Time	40 m

Nutritional Information:

Calories	336 kcal
Fat	18.2 g
Carbohydrates	38.7g
Protein	5 g
Cholesterol	104 mg
Sodium	114 mg

* Percent Daily Values are based on a 2,000 calorie diet.

PORTUGUESE DATE APPETIZER

Ingredients

- 1 lb sliced bacon
- 30 dates

Directions

- Cut your pieces of bacon in half then wrap your dates with them.
- Now stake a toothpick through each to preserve the structure.
- Cook the dates under the broiler for 7 mins with a broiler pan.
- Now flip each date and brown the opposite side.
- Enjoy.

Amount per serving (10 total)

Timing Information:

Preparation	10 m
Cooking	30 m
Total Time	40 m

Nutritional Information:

Calories	278 kcal
Fat	20.5 g
Carbohydrates	19g
Protein	5.9 g
Cholesterol	31 mg
Sodium	379 mg

* Percent Daily Values are based on a 2,000 calorie diet.

CALDO VERDE

Ingredients

- 4 tbsps olive oil, divided
- 1 onion, minced
- 1 clove garlic, minced
- 6 potatoes, peeled and thinly sliced
- 2 quarts cold water
- 6 oz. linguica sausage, thinly sliced
- 2 1/2 tsps salt
- ground black pepper to taste
- 1 lb kale, rinsed and julienned

Directions

- Stir fry your garlic and onions, in olive oil, in a big pot, for 5 mins.
- Now add the potatoes and continue cooking for 5 more mins before adding the water.

- Get everything boiling and cook the potatoes for 22 mins.
- At the same time stir fry your sausage for 12 mins then remove any excess oils.
- Once the potatoes are done mash them in a food processor, then add them back into the pot with the sausage and some pepper and salt.
- Get the soup hot again, place a lid on the pot, and cook everything for 7 mins.
- Now add the kale and cook the mix for 7 more mins then add some olive oil.
- Enjoy.

Amount per serving (6 total)

Timing Information:

Preparation	20 m
Cooking	30 m
Total Time	1 h

Nutritional Information:

Calories	402 kcal
Fat	20.2 g
Carbohydrates	45.2g
Protein	11.7 g
Cholesterol	25 mg
Sodium	1352 mg

* Percent Daily Values are based on a 2,000 calorie diet.

KALE SOUP FROM PORTUGAL

Ingredients

- 1/2 lb dried white pea beans
- 1/2 lb chorizo sausage, thinly sliced
- 1 lb beef soup bones
- 1 quart water
- 1 medium head cabbage, diced
- 2 bunches kale - rinsed, dried and diced
- 5 potatoes, peeled and cubed
- 1 quart hot water or as needed
- salt and pepper to taste

Directions

- Let your beans sit submerged in water throughout the night.
- Cook the following for 65 mins: 1 qt. of water, beans, soup bones, and chorizo.

- Now add in: potatoes, kale, and cabbage.
- Pour in more water to submerge the contents and cook everything for 25 more mins before adding some pepper and salt.
- Enjoy.

Amount per serving (10 total)

Timing Information:

Preparation	
Cooking	1 h 30 m
Total Time	8 h

Nutritional Information:

Calories	302 kcal
Fat	9.4 g
Carbohydrates	42.2g
Protein	14.9 g
Cholesterol	20 mg
Sodium	321 mg

* Percent Daily Values are based on a 2,000 calorie diet.

QUEIJADAS

(SWEET MUFFINS)

Ingredients

- 3 eggs
- 2 C. white sugar
- 3 tbsps butter
- 3/4 C. all-purpose flour
- 2 C. milk
- 1/2 tsp vanilla extract

Directions

- Coat a muffin tin with nonstick spray and then set your oven to 325 degrees before doing anything else.
- Now process the following in a food processor, until smooth: butter, eggs, and sugar.
- Add the milk and the flour then pulse the contents some more.

- Finally add the vanilla.
- Evenly distribute your batter throughout the muffin pan and cook everything in the oven for 50 mins.
- Enjoy.

Amount per serving (18 total)

Timing Information:

Preparation	10 m
Cooking	45 m
Total Time	55 m

Nutritional Information:

Calories	148 kcal
Fat	3.3 g
Carbohydrates	27.5g
Protein	2.5 g
Cholesterol	38 mg
Sodium	37 mg

* Percent Daily Values are based on a 2,000 calorie diet.

EASY PORTUGUESE BREAD

Ingredients

- 2 C. all-purpose flour
- 3 tsps baking powder
- 1/2 tsp salt
- 2 tbsps white sugar
- 3/4 C. milk
- 1 quart vegetable oil for frying

Directions

- Get a bowl, combine: sugar, flour, salt, and baking powder.
- Combine in the milk and stir the contents into a dough.
- Shape the mix into small balls. Then flatten them on a working surface.
- Each piece should have half an inch of thickness.
- Now fry everything in hot oil until brown, then flip, and fry again.

- Enjoy.

Amount per serving (16 total)

Timing Information:

Preparation	15 m
Cooking	15 m
Total Time	30 m

Nutritional Information:

Calories	118 kcal
Fat	5.9 g
Carbohydrates	14.3g
Protein	2 g
Cholesterol	< 1 mg
Sodium	< 169 mg

* Percent Daily Values are based on a 2,000 calorie diet.

MALASADAS

(SUGARY FRIED PASTRIES)

Ingredients

- 1 (.25 oz.) package active dry yeast
- 1 tsp white sugar
- 1/4 C. warm water (110 degrees F/45 degrees C)
- 6 eggs
- 6 C. all-purpose flour
- 1/2 C. white sugar
- 1/4 C. butter, melted
- 1 C. evaporated milk
- 1 C. water
- 1 tsp salt
- 2 quarts vegetable oil for frying
- 2 C. white sugar

Directions

`

- Get a bowl, combine: a quarter of a C. of warm water, 1 tsp sugar, and yeast.
- Get a 2nd bowl and whisk your eggs in it.
- Get a 3rd bowl for your flour.
- Create an opening in the middle of the flour and add the following in the center: salt, yeast mix, 1 C. water, eggs, milk, half C. sugar, and melted butter.
- Form everything into a dough and place a towel over the bowl.
- Let the dough rise until it has become twice its original size.
- Now get your oil hot for frying about 375 degrees and fry your dough in tbsp sized dollops until browned.
- Once you have finished one batch place them in a bowl with sugar and shake the contents.
- Enjoy.

Amount per serving (84 total)

Timing Information:

Preparation	10 m
Cooking	40 m
Total Time	50 m

Nutritional Information:

Calories	88 kcal
Fat	3.3 g
Carbohydrates	13.2g
Protein	1.6 g
Cholesterol	16 mg
Sodium	40 mg

* Percent Daily Values are based on a 2,000 calorie diet.

Spicy Spanish Beef Stir Fry

Ingredients

- 3/4 C. red wine
- 1/4 C. water
- 10 cloves garlic, diced
- 1 tbsp chili paste
- 1/2 tsp white pepper
- 1/2 tsp salt
- 6 (4 oz.) beef tenderloin steaks
- 1/3 C. vegetable oil

Directions

- Get a bowl, combine: salt, wine, white pepper, beef, water, chili paste, and garlic.
- Mix everything to make sure the beef is covered with seasonings.
- Fry your beef for 3 mins per side then place them to the side.
- Pour the beef drippings into the wine mix and add the beef back

into the pan and fry everything
for 3 more mins with additional
oil.
- Combine the wine mix with the
  beef and get everything boiling.
- Let the contents cook for 5 mins.
- Enjoy.

Amount per serving (6 total)

Timing Information:

Preparation	10 m
Cooking	20 m
Total Time	30 m

Nutritional Information:

Calories	467 kcal
Fat	38.6 g
Carbohydrates	4g
Protein	20.5 g
Cholesterol	81 mg
Sodium	272 mg

* Percent Daily Values are based on a 2,000 calorie diet.

MAGGIE'S EASY PORTUGUESE SOUP

Ingredients

- 1/4 C. vegetable oil
- 2 C. diced onion
- 1 lb smoked sausage, sliced
- 1 medium head cabbage, diced
- 6 potatoes, peeled and cubed
- 2 (15 oz.) cans kidney beans
- 2 C. ketchup
- 1 (10.5 oz.) can beef consommé
- 2 2/3 quarts water
- 2 tsps garlic powder
- 2 tsps ground black pepper
- 1 tsp salt
- 1/2 C. vinegar

Directions

- Stir fry your onions until soft then add in the sausage and cook everything for 7 more mins.

- Now add: water, salt, cabbage, pepper, consommé, potatoes, garlic powder, ketchup, and beans.
- Get everything boiling, set the heat to low, and cook the contents for 40 mins.
- Now add the vinegar and continue cooking for 65 more mins.
- Enjoy.

Amount per serving (8 total)

Timing Information:

Preparation	20 m
Cooking	1 h 30 m
Total Time	1 h 50 m

Nutritional Information:

Calories	537 kcal
Fat	19.9 g
Carbohydrates	73.3g
Protein	20.7 g
Cholesterol	37 mg
Sodium	2127 mg

* Percent Daily Values are based on a 2,000 calorie diet.

GARBANZO AND CABBAGE SOUP

Ingredients

- 1 medium onion, diced
- 3 cloves garlic, minced
- 4 tbsps olive oil
- 1 lb Portuguese chourico, broken into large chunks
- 2 (15 oz.) cans kidney beans, drained
- 1 (15 oz.) can garbanzo beans, drained
- 5 Yukon Gold potatoes, cubed
- 2 pork chops
- salt and pepper
- 3 tbsps Pimenta Moida (Portuguese hot diced peppers)
- 1 bunch kale - washed, dried, and shredded
- 1/2 head savoy cabbage, shredded

Directions

- Stir fry your garlic and onions in olive oil until tender then add the pork, chourico, potatoes, and beans.
- Add in the water to submerge everything and also some pepper and salt.
- Get everything boiling then set the heat to low and cook the mix until you find that the potatoes are soft.
- Add in some more pepper and salt and also the pimento.
- Continue cooking the mix for 2 more mins then add the cabbage and kale.
- Now turn up the heat and boil everything for 7 mins.
- Enjoy.

Amount per serving (12 total)

Timing Information:

Preparation	10 m
Cooking	30 m
Total Time	50 m

Nutritional Information:

Calories	348 kcal
Fat	17.1 g
Carbohydrates	33g
Protein	17.3 g
Cholesterol	36 mg
Sodium	618 mg

* Percent Daily Values are based on a 2,000 calorie diet.

RICE FROM PORTUGAL

Ingredients

- 1 1/2 quarts milk
- 1 C. uncooked white rice
- 1 C. white sugar
- 2 eggs, beaten

Directions

- Heat your milk and sugar until it is bubbly. Then add the rice and cook the mix for 65 mins with a low heat.
- The contents should not be boiling during this time.
- Now shut the heat and add in the whisked eggs gradually.
- Enjoy.

Amount per serving (8 total)

Timing Information:

Preparation	5 m
Cooking	1 h
Total Time	1 h 5 m

Nutritional Information:

Calories	296 kcal
Fat	5 g
Carbohydrates	53.2g
Protein	9.5 g
Cholesterol	61 mg
Sodium	93 mg

* Percent Daily Values are based on a 2,000 calorie diet.

Restaurant Style Clams I

Ingredients

- 5 lbs clams in shell, scrubbed clean, remove any which are opened
- 1 1/2 lbs chorizo, sliced into chunks
- 1 large onion, cut into thin wedges
- 1 (14.5 oz.) can diced tomatoes
- 2 C. white wine
- 1/4 C. olive oil

Directions

- Add the following to a big pot: clams, wine, sausage, tomatoes, and onions.
- Place a lid on the pot and cook the mix with a high level of heat until your clams open.

- When all the clams have opened add some olive oil and serve the dish in soup bowls with a liberal amount of broth.
- Enjoy.

Amount per serving (6 total)

Timing Information:

Preparation	30 m
Cooking	20 m
Total Time	50 m

Nutritional Information:

Calories	697 kcal
Fat	52.6 g
Carbohydrates	9.1g
Protein	29.9 g
Cholesterol	104 mg
Sodium	1567 mg

* Percent Daily Values are based on a 2,000 calorie diet.

SPANISH SAUSAGE AND PEPPERS

Ingredients

- 2 lbs chorizo sausage, casings removed and crumbled
- 2 green bell peppers, seeded and diced
- 2 sweet onion, peeled and diced
- 1 (6 oz.) can tomato paste
- 1 C. red wine
- 1 C. water
- 2 tbsps crushed garlic

Directions

- Add the following to your crock pot: garlic, sausage, water, green pepper, wine, onions, and tomato paste.
- Place a lid on the pot, after stirring the contents, and cook the mix for 8 hrs with low heat.

- Enjoy the dish over cooked yellow rice.

Amount per serving (8 total)

Timing Information:

Preparation	15 m
Cooking	10 h
Total Time	10 h 15 m

Nutritional Information:

Calories	579 kcal
Fat	43.6 g
Carbohydrates	11.5g
Protein	29 g
Cholesterol	100 mg
Sodium	1574 mg

* Percent Daily Values are based on a 2,000 calorie diet.

COUNTRYSIDE PORTUGUESE POTATOES AND WINE

Ingredients

- 2 tbsps extra-virgin olive oil
- 1 lb beef stew meat, cut into cubes
- 1 tbsp all-purpose flour
- 8 cloves garlic, minced
- 2 bay leaves
- 1 pinch ground black pepper
- 1 pinch salt
- 1 onion, diced
- 1 green bell pepper, diced
- 1 carrot, diced
- 1 pinch paprika
- 1/2 fresh tomato, diced
- 1 C. white wine
- 1 C. water
- 2 sprigs fresh parsley
- 3 red potatoes, peeled and cubed
- 1 sweet potato, peeled and cubed
- 1 (14.5 oz.) can green beans, drained

Directions

- Coat your beef with flour and then add the following to a large pot with oil: pepper, beef, bay leaves, and garlic.
- Once the beef is browned all over, about 7 mins of frying, add some salt.
- Now add: paprika, onion, carrots, and green pepper.
- Cook the onion mix for 7 mins. Then add: parsley, tomato, water, and wine.
- Place a lid on the pot and cook everything for 35 mins.
- Add the green beans and the sweet and red potatoes.
- Let the potatoes cook for 50 mins.
- Enjoy.

Amount per serving (6 total)

Timing Information:

Preparation	30 m
Cooking	1 h 30 m
Total Time	2 h

Nutritional Information:

Calories	398 kcal
Fat	12 g
Carbohydrates	37.9g
Protein	27.4 g
Cholesterol	65 mg
Sodium	279 mg

* Percent Daily Values are based on a 2,000 calorie diet.

FAVA BEANS SPANISH STYLE

Ingredients

- 5 tbsps olive oil
- 3 large onions, diced
- 2 cloves garlic, minced
- 2 tbsps red pepper flakes
- 1/4 C. tomato sauce
- 2 C. hot water
- 3 tbsps diced fresh parsley
- salt to taste
- 1/2 tsp black pepper
- 2 tsps paprika
- 2 (19 oz.) cans fava beans

Directions

- Stir fry your garlic and onions in oil until browned.
- Now add paprika, pepper flakes, pepper, tomato sauce, salt, parsley, and hot water.

- Get the mix boiling, set the heat to low, and cook everything for 35 mins.
- Now add in your beans and shut the heat.
- Let the beans sit in the mix for 15 mins with a lid on the pot.
- Enjoy.

Amount per serving (8 total)

Timing Information:

Preparation	15 m
Cooking	30 m
Total Time	45 m

Nutritional Information:

Calories	221 kcal
Fat	9.5 g
Carbohydrates	27.7g
Protein	7.4 g
Cholesterol	0 mg
Sodium	300 mg

* Percent Daily Values are based on a 2,000 calorie diet.

LINGUICA SOUP

Ingredients

- 1 ham hock
- 1 (10 oz.) linguica sausage, sliced
- 1 onion, minced
- 2 quarts water
- 4 potatoes, peeled and cubed
- 2 celery rib, diced
- 2 carrots, diced
- 1 (15 oz.) can stewed tomatoes
- 1 (8 oz.) can tomato sauce
- 1 clove garlic, minced
- 1/2 head cabbage, thinly sliced
- 1 (15 oz.) can kidney beans

Directions

- Get the following boiling in a big pot: water, ham hock, onions, and linguica.
- Place a lid on the pot and cook everything for 65 mins.

- Take out the ham hock and take off all of the meat.
- Dice this meat and place it back into the pot along with: garlic, potatoes, tomato sauce, celery, stewed tomatoes, and carrots.
- Place the lid on the pot again and cook everything for 90 mins.
- Stir the contents every 10 to 15 mins.
- Now add the beans and the cabbage.
- Cook this mix for 12 mins then serve.
- Enjoy.

Amount per serving (12 total)

Timing Information:

Preparation	10 m
Cooking	2 h 40 m
Total Time	2 h 50 m

Nutritional Information:

Calories	268 kcal
Fat	12.9 g
Carbohydrates	25.6g
Protein	13.3 g
Cholesterol	32 mg
Sodium	581 mg

* Percent Daily Values are based on a 2,000 calorie diet.

Rice Casserole

Ingredients

- 3 C. water
- 1 1/2 C. uncooked white rice
- 1 tbsp butter
- 1 tbsp olive oil
- 1 tbsp olive oil
- 1 small onion, diced
- 2 cloves garlic, minced
- 2 (5 oz.) cans tuna, drained
- 3/4 C. heavy cream
- 3 tbsps ketchup
- 1 tsp hot pepper sauce
- salt and pepper to taste
- 1/2 C. sliced black olives
- 1/2 C. shredded Cheddar cheese

Directions

- Get the following boiling: 1 tbsp of olive oil, rice, butter, and water.

- Once the mix is boiling, place a lid on the pot, and set the heat to a low level. Cook the rice for 27 mins.
- Now set your oven to 350 degrees before doing anything else.
- Stir fry your onions and garlic in 1 tbsp of olive oil for 7 mins then add the following: pepper, tuna, salt, hot sauce, ketchup, and cream.
- Cook the contents for 12 mins.
- Now add half of your rice to a casserole dish then top it with the tuna then add the rest of the rice.
- Coat the layers with cheese and olives.
- Cook the casserole in the oven for 25 mins.
- Enjoy.

Amount per serving (6 total)

Timing Information:

Preparation	15 m
Cooking	45 m
Total Time	1 h

Nutritional Information:

Calories	442 kcal
Fat	22.5 g
Carbohydrates	42g
Protein	17.4 g
Cholesterol	68 mg
Sodium	318 mg

* Percent Daily Values are based on a 2,000 calorie diet.

CACOILA

(PORTUGUESE BEEF)

Ingredients

- 2 lbs beef stew meat, cleaned, cut into 1 inch cubes
- 3 oranges, juiced
- 1/4 C. white wine
- 1 tsp hot pepper sauce
- 1 tsp vegetable oil
- 2 bay leaves
- 2 cloves garlic, crushed
- 1 tsp paprika
- 1/4 tsp ground allspice
- salt and ground black pepper to taste

Directions

- Get a bowl, add the following: pepper, pepper sauce, garlic, salt, orange juice, allspice, oil, paprika, bay leaves, and wine.

- Place a covering on the bowl and put it all in the fridge for 8 hrs.
- Now cook your beef and the sauce for 65 mins in a large pot.
- Enjoy.

Amount per serving (6 total)

Timing Information:

Preparation	30 m
Cooking	1 h
Total Time	14 h

Nutritional Information:

Calories	437 kcal
Fat	30 g
Carbohydrates	10.8g
Protein	28.5 g
Cholesterol	101 mg
Sodium	91 mg

* Percent Daily Values are based on a 2,000 calorie diet.

CHICKEN SOUP FROM SPAIN

Ingredients

- 1 whole bone-in chicken breast, with skin
- 1 onion, cut into thin wedges
- 4 sprigs fresh parsley
- 1/2 tsp lemon zest
- 1 sprig fresh mint
- 6 C. chicken stock
- 1/3 C. thin egg noodles
- 2 tbsps diced fresh mint leaves
- salt to taste
- 1/4 tsp freshly ground white pepper

Directions

- Gently boil the following for 40 mins: mint sprig, chicken breast, lemon zest, parsley, and onions.
- Take out the chicken and cut it into strips.

- Now run the broth through a strainer and add it back to the pot.
- Get the broth boiling, then add the diced mint and the pasta.
- Add some white pepper and salt as well.
- Cook the pasta for about 9 mins then shut the heat and add in: chicken and lemon juice.
- Divide the soup amongst your serving dishes and garnish each one with mint and a piece of lemon.
- Enjoy.

Amount per serving (4 total)

Timing Information:

Preparation	10 m
Cooking	1 h
Total Time	1 h 10 m

Nutritional Information:

Calories	159 kcal
Fat	7.1 g
Carbohydrates	6.8g
Protein	16.8 g
Cholesterol	49 mg
Sodium	63 mg

* Percent Daily Values are based on a 2,000 calorie diet.

CAJUN PEPPERS AND RED BEANS

Ingredients

- 1 tbsp olive oil
- 8 oz. bacon, cooked and cubed
- 1 1/2 C. diced onion
- 1/4 C. diced green bell pepper
- 1 tbsp minced garlic
- 4 bay leaves
- 6 oz. sliced andouille sausage
- 1 small smoked ham hock
- 2 C. dry kidney beans, soaked overnight
- 1 tsp Cajun seasoning
- 1 tsp Worcestershire sauce
- 8 C. chicken broth
- 1 tsp salt
- 1 1/2 C. cooked rice
- 6 tbsps thinly sliced green onion

Directions

- Stir fry your bacon for 4 mins in very hot oil then add in: ham hock, onion, sausage, bell pepper, bay leaves, and garlic. Cook this mix for 3 more mins.
- Now add the beans and fry them for 3 mins.
- Add in: stock, Worcestershire and the Cajun seasoning.
- Get the mix boiling, set the heat to low, and cook the contents for 60 mins.
- Now add in some salt, place a lid on the pot, and continue cooking everything for 17 more mins.
- Now shut the heat and let the contents stand for 25 mins.
- Remove the ham hock and throw it away.
- Divide the soup into serving dishes and add a quarter of a C. of rice to each and well as some green onions.
- Enjoy.

Amount per serving (6 total)

Timing Information:

Preparation	10 m
Cooking	1 h
Total Time	1 h 10 m

Nutritional Information:

Calories	671 kcal
Fat	36 g
Carbohydrates	54.9g
Protein	31.9 g
Cholesterol	67 mg
Sodium	1240 mg

* Percent Daily Values are based on a 2,000 calorie diet.

SPANISH CLAMS

Ingredients

- 24 small clams in shell, scrubbed
- 1/4 C. cornmeal
- 1/4 C. olive oil
- 3 cloves garlic, minced
- 8 oz. chourico sausage, diced
- 1 medium red onion, sliced
- 1 pinch red pepper flakes (optional)
- 1 (12 fluid oz.) can or bottle dark beer
- 1 (8 oz.) bottle clam juice
- 1 (28 oz.) can crushed roma tomatoes
- 3 tbsps diced fresh oregano
- 1 pinch salt and pepper to taste

Directions

- Submerge your clams in water, in a saucepan, then add the cornmeal.
- Let the contents sit for 25 mins then run the clams until water.
- Stir fry your garlic in olive oil for 5 mins then add: red pepper flakes, chourico, and onions.
- Cook the mix for 4 mins. Then add your beer and let the mix cook for 5 mins.
- Now add in the clams, tomatoes, and clam juice.
- Place a lid on the pan and cook the contents until the clams open.
- Add pepper, salt, and oregano.
- Enjoy.

Amount per serving (4 total)

Timing Information:

Preparation	10 m
Cooking	20 m
Total Time	30 m

Nutritional Information:

Calories	435 kcal
Fat	30.5 g
Carbohydrates	23.2g
Protein	12.9 g
Cholesterol	46 mg
Sodium	910 mg

* Percent Daily Values are based on a 2,000 calorie diet.

Portuguese Green Soup

Ingredients

- 3 tbsps olive oil
- 1 onion, finely diced
- 3 cloves garlic, crushed
- 6 potatoes, peeled and thinly sliced
- 1 lb cabbage, thinly sliced
- 2 quarts water
- 8 oz. Portuguese chourico sausage, casing removed, sliced 1/4-inch thick
- 1 tsp smoked paprika
- 2 tsps salt
- pepper to taste
- olive oil

Directions

- Stir fry your garlic and onions in 3 tbsps of olive oil for 5 mins then add half of your cabbage and the potatoes.

- Cook the cabbage for 5 mins.
- Add the water and get everything boiling.
- Place a lid on the pot and let the contents gently boil over medium heat for 17 mins.
- Now with an immersion blender puree the soup.
- Then get everything hot again.
- Add in the rest of the cabbage, the sausage, some pepper, salt, and paprika.
- Get the mix simmering and then place the lid back on the pot.
- Cook the contents for 7 mins.
- Divide the soup between your serving bowls and top everything with some olive oil
- Enjoy.

Amount per serving (6 total)

Timing Information:

Preparation	30 m
Cooking	40 m
Total Time	1 h 10 m

Nutritional Information:

Calories	456 kcal
Fat	27 g
Carbohydrates	44.7g
Protein	11 g
Cholesterol	26 mg
Sodium	1144 mg

* Percent Daily Values are based on a 2,000 calorie diet.

Restaurant Style Rabbit

Ingredients

- 1 (2 lb) rabbit, cleaned and cut into pieces
- salt and pepper to taste
- 3 tbsps prepared mustard
- 3 tbsps vegetable oil
- 1 C. white wine
- 4 small onions
- 2 slices bacon, cut into 1/2 inch pieces
- 1 orange

Directions

- Set your oven to 350 degrees before doing anything else.
- Coat your rabbit with some pepper and salt. Then top it evenly with mustard.
- Combine the seasoned meat, in a Dutch oven, with wine and oil.

- Then add the onions and the bacon.
- Cook the contents in the oven for 35 mins with the lid on the pot then flip the meat and add some squeezed orange juice.
- Cook everything for 35 more mins without the lid.
- Enjoy with cooked mashed potato.

Amount per serving (4 total)

Timing Information:

Preparation	15 m
Cooking	1 h
Total Time	1 h 15 m

Nutritional Information:

Calories	570 kcal
Fat	29.7 g
Carbohydrates	13.8g
Protein	48.9 g
Cholesterol	139 mg
Sodium	347 mg

* Percent Daily Values are based on a 2,000 calorie diet.

Brazilian Chorizo Soup

Ingredients

- 1 tbsp canola oil
- 1/4 lb chorizo sausage, diced
- 1/3 lb cooked ham, diced
- 1 medium onion, diced
- 2 cloves garlic, minced
- 2 (1 lb) sweet potatoes, peeled and diced
- 1 large red bell pepper, diced
- 2 (14.5 oz.) cans diced tomatoes with juice
- 1 small hot green chile pepper, diced
- 1 1/2 C. water
- 2 (16 oz.) cans black beans, rinsed and drained
- 1 mango - peeled, seeded and diced
- 1/4 C. diced fresh cilantro
- 1/4 tsp salt

Directions

- Stir fry your ham and chorizo for 5 mins then add the garlic and onions.
- Fry them until they are soft.
- Add in: water, sweet potatoes, chili pepper, bell peppers, and tomatoes and liquid.
- Get everything boiling then place a lid on the pot, set the heat to low, and let the contents cook for 17 mins.
- Now add the beans and heat them with no cover.
- Once the beans are hot add the cilantro and mango.
- Enjoy.

Amount per serving (6 total)

Timing Information:

Preparation	15 m
Cooking	30 m
Total Time	45 m

Nutritional Information:

Calories	508 kcal
Fat	15 g
Carbohydrates	70.7g
Protein	22.8 g
Cholesterol	31 mg
Sodium	1538 mg

* Percent Daily Values are based on a 2,000 calorie diet.

SOUTH AMERICAN BANANA PIE

Ingredients

- 3 tbsps brown sugar
- 1/2 C. water
- 10 bananas, peeled and sliced lengthwise
- 2 C. whole wheat flour
- 2 C. toasted wheat germ
- 3 C. rolled oats
- 1 C. packed brown sugar
- 1 C. light margarine
- 1 tbsp cinnamon

Directions

- Set your oven to 350 degrees before doing anything else.
- In a saucepan add in 3 tbsps of brown sugar and heat it until it melts. Then add some water and stir everything until the sugar and water are completely combined.

- Add this syrup to a pie dish and cover the bottom. Now layer a covering of bananas.
- Get a bowl, combine: 1 C. brown sugar, margarine, wheat flour, oats, and wheat germ.
- Now with your hands make a dough that is somewhat crumbly.
- Add 1/2 of this mix over the bananas then add the rest of the bananas and top them with cinnamon.
- Press everything down and add the rest of the dough.
- Cook the contents in the oven for 50 mins.
- Enjoy.

Amount per serving (12 total)

Timing Information:

Preparation	20 m
Cooking	45 m
Total Time	1 h 5 m

Nutritional Information:

Calories	451 kcal
Fat	11.2 g
Carbohydrates	82.5g
Protein	11.1 g
Cholesterol	0 mg
Sodium	126 mg

* Percent Daily Values are based on a 2,000 calorie diet.

Canja

(Portuguese Chicken Soup)

Ingredients

- 3 lbs boneless, skinless chicken meat
- 1 onion, diced
- 6 C. chicken stock
- 1/4 C. long-grain white rice
- 3/4 C. tomato - peeled, seeded and diced
- 1/2 C. diced carrots
- salt to taste
- ground black pepper to taste
- 3/4 C. diced ham
- 1 tbsp diced fresh parsley

Directions

- Get the following boiling: stock, onions, and chicken.

- Once the mix is boiling, place a lid on the pot, set the heat to low, and cook the contents with a low level of heat for 50 mins.
- Place the chicken to the side and run the broth through a strainer.
- Keep only the broth and throw away everything else.
- Clean the pan and add the stock back in as well as the rice, carrots, tomatoes, pepper and salt.
- Get the contents boiling again and lower the heat to a low level and cook the rice for 37 mins.
- At the same time begin to julienne the meat of your chicken then add the chicken to the soup with the ham and some parsley.
- Enjoy.

Amount per serving (6 total)

Timing Information:

Preparation	10 m
Cooking	1 h 30 m
Total Time	1 h 40 m

Nutritional Information:

Calories	507 kcal
Fat	27.2 g
Carbohydrates	11.4g
Protein	50.4 g
Cholesterol	1165 mg
Sodium	1306 mg

* Percent Daily Values are based on a 2,000 calorie diet.

SPANISH GREENS

Ingredients

- 1/2 lb peppered bacon, diced
- 1 onion, diced
- 2 lbs collard greens - rinsed, stemmed and torn into 3x6 inch pieces
- 1 C. chicken stock
- 1 tsp cayenne pepper
- 2 tbsps red wine vinegar

Directions

- Stir fry your bacon until fully done then add the onions and cook them for 6 mins. Add the greens then add the stock and cayenne.
- Get the mix boiling and set the heat to low.
- Cook everything for 80 mins.

- Now add in the wine vinegar and cook for 17 more mins until half of the juices have evaporated.
- Enjoy.

Amount per serving (6 total)

Timing Information:

Preparation	10 m
Cooking	2 h
Total Time	2 h 10 m

Nutritional Information:

Calories	269 kcal
Fat	19.4 g
Carbohydrates	10.1g
Protein	15.1 g
Cholesterol	32 mg
Sodium	744 mg

* Percent Daily Values are based on a 2,000 calorie diet.

MAGGIE'S FAVORITE BRAZILIAN RIBS

Ingredients

- 10 pork spareribs
- 1/2 C. soy sauce
- 10 cloves garlic, crushed
- 1 tbsp dried rosemary
- 1 tbsp dried oregano
- 2 bay leaves
- 1 lime, juiced
- 10 sprigs fresh parsley
- ground black pepper to taste
- 2 limes, cut into wedges

Directions

- Submerge your ribs, in water, in a saucepan.
- Now add: 3/4 parsley, soy sauce, lime juice, garlic, bay leaves, oregano, and rosemary.

- Get everything boiling then set the heat to a medium level and cook the contents for 30 mins until no liquid remains.
- Now take out the leaves and brown the meat.
- Scrape the bottom of the pan and stir the contents.
- Cook everything for about 7 more mins.
- Then add some pepper, a topping of lime pieces, and the rest of the parsley when serving.
- Enjoy.

Amount per serving (6 total)

Timing Information:

Preparation	10 m
Cooking	40 m
Total Time	1 h

Nutritional Information:

Calories	461 kcal
Fat	32 g
Carbohydrates	10.7g
Protein	33.5 g
Cholesterol	125 mg
Sodium	1327 mg

* Percent Daily Values are based on a 2,000 calorie diet.

South American Tilapia Stew

Ingredients

- 3 tbsps lime juice
- 1 tbsp ground cumin
- 1 tbsp paprika
- 2 tsps minced garlic
- 1 tsp salt
- 1 tsp ground black pepper
- 1 1/2 lbs tilapia fillets, cut into chunks
- 2 tbsps olive oil
- 2 onions, diced
- 4 large bell peppers, sliced
- 1 (16 oz.) can diced tomatoes, drained
- 1 (16 oz.) can coconut milk
- 1 bunch fresh cilantro, diced (optional)

Directions

- Get a bowl, combine: tilapia, pepper, lime juice, salt, cumin, garlic, and paprika.
- Stir the contents to evenly coat the fish and then place everything in the fridge for 60 mins.
- Now begin to fry your onions in olive oil for 3 mins then reduce the heat to a medium level.
- Add in the bell pepper, diced tomatoes, and seasoned fish.
- Cook the contents for 1 min then add the coconut milk.
- Place a lid on the pot and cook the contents for 20 mins with a medium heat.
- Stir the mix at least 2 times then add the cilantro and cook everything for 7 more mins.
- Enjoy.

Amount per serving (6 total)

Timing Information:

Preparation	20 m
Cooking	25 m
Total Time	1 h 5 m

Nutritional Information:

Calories	359 kcal
Fat	21.8 g
Carbohydrates	15.6g
Protein	27.4 g
Cholesterol	42 mg
Sodium	600 mg

* Percent Daily Values are based on a 2,000 calorie diet.

EASY BRAZILIAN RICE

Ingredients

- 2 C. long-grain white rice, rinses and dried
- 2 tbsps minced onion
- 2 cloves garlic, minced
- 2 tbsps vegetable oil
- 1 tsp salt
- 4 C. hot water

Directions

- Stir fry your onions in oil for 3 mins then add the garlic and cook the garlic until it is brown.
- Now add the salt and the rice.
- Toast the rice for a few mins until it is slightly browned then add the hot water.
- Place a lid on the pot and cook the rice with a low level of heat for 23 mins.

- Enjoy.

Amount per serving (8 total)

Timing Information:

Preparation	15 m
Cooking	30 m
Total Time	45 m

Nutritional Information:

Calories	201 kcal
Fat	3.7 g
Carbohydrates	37.5g
Protein	3.4 g
Cholesterol	0 mg
Sodium	297 mg

* Percent Daily Values are based on a
2,000 calorie diet.

Frango e Coconuts

(Coconut Chicken)

Ingredients

- 1 tsp ground cumin
- 1 tsp ground cayenne pepper
- 1 tsp ground turmeric
- 1 tsp ground coriander
- 4 skinless, boneless chicken breast halves
- salt and pepper to taste
- 2 tbsps olive oil
- 1 onion, diced
- 1 tbsp minced fresh ginger
- 2 jalapeno peppers, seeded and diced
- 2 cloves garlic, minced
- 3 tomatoes, seeded and diced
- 1 (14 oz.) can light coconut milk
- 1 bunch diced fresh parsley

Directions

- Get a bowl, combine: coriander, cumin, turmeric, and cayenne.
- Now add in the chicken and also some pepper and salt.
- Stir the contents to evenly coat the chicken pieces.
- Now begin to stir fry your chicken in 1 tbsp of olive oil until fully done, for 16 mins. Place the chicken to the side.
- Add in the rest of the oil and begin to fry the following for 7 mins: garlic, onion, jalapenos, and ginger.
- Add the tomatoes and cook the mix for 10 more mins before pouring in the coconut milk.
- Top the chicken with the tomato and coconut mix and then some parsley.
- Enjoy.

Amount per serving (4 total)

Timing Information:

Preparation	15 m
Cooking	30 m
Total Time	45 m

Nutritional Information:

Calories	345 kcal
Fat	19.9 g
Carbohydrates	11.5g
Protein	29.3 g
Cholesterol	72 mg
Sodium	234 mg

* Percent Daily Values are based on a 2,000 calorie diet.

Brazilian Orange and Bean Soup

Ingredients

- 1 tbsp olive oil
- 3 C. onion, diced
- 8 cloves garlic, diced, divided
- 1 carrot, diced
- 3 tsps ground cumin
- 2 tsps salt
- 1 red bell pepper, diced
- 2 (15 oz.) cans black beans, drained and rinsed
- 1/2 C. water
- 1 C. orange juice
- 1 pinch cayenne pepper, or to taste

Directions

- Stir fry your carrots, half of the garlic, and the onions in olive oil until soft. Then add in the salt and cumin.

- Cook everything for 1 more min before adding in the red pepper and the rest of the garlic.
- Cook the new garlic until it is soft.
- Now add: orange juice, cayenne, water, and beans.
- Now grab an immersion blender and puree the entire mix until it reaches a consistency you enjoy without any heating.
- Heat everything back up after you have pureed it and continue cooking for 12 mins.
- Enjoy.

Amount per serving (6 total)

Timing Information:

Preparation	30 m
Cooking	30 m
Total Time	1 h

Nutritional Information:

Calories	80 kcal
Fat	2.7 g
Carbohydrates	13.3g
Protein	1.7 g
Cholesterol	0 mg
Sodium	788 mg

* Percent Daily Values are based on a 2,000 calorie diet.

PORTUGUESE PORK STEW

Ingredients

- 2 tbsps vegetable oil
- 1 tsp minced garlic
- 1 large onion, diced
- 1 (12 oz.) pork tenderloin, cut into 1/2 inch cubes
- 1 (19 oz.) can black beans, drained and rinsed
- 1/4 C. water
- 1 1/2 C. chicken stock
- 3 chorizo sausages, cut into 1/2 inch thick pieces
- 2 bay leaves
- salt and pepper to taste

Directions

- Stir fry your onions and garlic in 1 tbsp of veggie oil for 5 mins then add 1 more tsp of oil then the pork.

- Cook the pork until browned all over with a high level of heat.
- At the same time blend the following: 1/4 C. of water, 3/4 of the beans.
- Now add the puree and the rest of the beans to the pork and also add: bay leaves, chorizo, and stock.
- Get everything boiling, place a lid on the pot, and let the contents cook for 35 mins.
- Add in some pepper, salt and the chorizo mix to serving bowls.
- Enjoy.

Amount per serving (4 total)

Timing Information:

Preparation	20 m
Cooking	40 m
Total Time	1 h

Nutritional Information:

Calories	482 kcal
Fat	26.7 g
Carbohydrates	27.4g
Protein	32.8 g
Cholesterol	77 mg
Sodium	1361 mg

* Percent Daily Values are based on a 2,000 calorie diet.

FEIJOADA II

(BRAZILIAN BEAN STEW)

Ingredients

- 1 (12 oz.) package dry black beans, soaked overnight
- 1 1/2 C. diced onion, divided
- 1/2 C. green onions, diced
- 1 clove garlic, diced
- 2 smoked ham hocks
- 8 oz. diced ham
- 1/2 lb thickly sliced bacon, diced
- 1 tbsp olive oil
- 2 bay leaves, crushed
- 1/8 tsp ground coriander
- salt and pepper to taste
- 1/2 C. diced fresh cilantro (optional)
- 1/4 C. diced fresh parsley (optional)

Directions

- For 6 mins stir fry the following in a Dutch oven: garlic, 3/4 C. onions, and green onions.
- Now add the beans and submerge everything in water with about 3 inches of extra.
- Get the mix boiling, set the heat to low and cook everything for two hrs.
- At the same time add your ham to a 2nd pot with 1/4 of the diced onions.
- Submerge the mix in water then cook everything for 65 mins.
- Remove the liquid and combine the ham with the beans.
- Now set your oven to 375 degrees before doing anything else.
- Layer the following in a casserole dish: the rest of the onions, the bacon, and ham.
- Cook this for 20 mins in the oven then remove any liquids before adding it to the beans.
- Also add in: pepper, bay leaves, coriander, and salt.

- Cook the mix for 35 more mins then add the parsley and cilantro.
- Enjoy.

Amount per serving (8 total)

Timing Information:

Preparation	30 m
Cooking	2 h 30 m
Total Time	11 h

Nutritional Information:

Calories	381 kcal
Fat	18 g
Carbohydrates	31g
Protein	24.1 g
Cholesterol	52 mg
Sodium	450 mg

* Percent Daily Values are based on a 2,000 calorie diet.

Picadinho'a

(Brazilian Ground Beef)

Ingredients

- 1/2 C. olive oil
- 2 onions, diced
- 4 cloves diced garlic
- 2 lbs ground beef
- 3 stalks celery, diced
- 1 green bell pepper, diced
- 6 eggs
- 1 (15.5 oz.) can diced tomatoes, with liquid
- 1 C. diced fresh parsley
- 1 1/2 C. red wine
- 1/4 tsp crushed red pepper flakes, or to taste

Directions

- Stir fry your garlic and onions in olive oil.

- Cook them for 17 mins while constantly stirring.
- At the same time get a bowl and mix: parsley, beef, tomatoes, celery, eggs, and bell pepper.
- Combine the beef with the onions and turn up the heat.
- Stir fry everything for 12 mins then set the heat to low and place a lid on the pot.
- Cook the mix for 17 more mins then add the pepper flakes and the red wine.
- Gently boil the contents with a low heat for 60 more mins.
- Enjoy.

Amount per serving (8 total)

Timing Information:

Preparation	30 m
Cooking	1 h 40 m
Total Time	2 h 10 m

Nutritional Information:

Calories	449 kcal
Fat	31.1 g
Carbohydrates	8g
Protein	25.2 g
Cholesterol	211 mg
Sodium	223 mg

* Percent Daily Values are based on a 2,000 calorie diet.

A Dessert from Brazil

(Banana and Coconut Bake)

Ingredients

- 6 medium bananas, halved lengthwise
- 1/2 C. fresh orange juice
- 1 tbsp fresh lemon juice
- 1/2 C. white sugar
- 1/8 tsp salt
- 2 tbsps butter
- 1 C. flaked coconut

Directions

- Coat a casserole dish with butter and then set your oven to 400 degrees before doing anything else.
- Get a bowl, combine: salt, orange juice, sugar, and lemon juice.

- Add the bananas to the casserole dish and top them with the lemon juice mix.
- Now spread pieces of butter throughout.
- Cook the bananas for 17 mins in the oven then garnish them with coconut.
- Enjoy.

Amount per serving (12 total)

Timing Information:

Preparation	15 m
Cooking	15 m
Total Time	30 m

Nutritional Information:

Calories	135 kcal
Fat	3.9 g
Carbohydrates	26.2g
Protein	0.9 g
Cholesterol	5 mg
Sodium	56 mg

* Percent Daily Values are based on a
2,000 calorie diet.

EASY RIBS FROM BRAZIL

Ingredients

- 1 (3 lb) rack of whole beef ribs, fat removed
- 2 tbsps sea salt, or more if needed
- 3/4 C. water

Directions

- Set your oven to 275 degrees before doing anything else.
- Coat your beef with a generous amount of sea salt all over.
- Then cook the meat in the oven for 6 hrs.
- Baste the meat with beef broth after 60 mins has elapsed.
- Continue basting every 60 mins. Then let the beef sit for 17 mins then cut it up.
- Enjoy.

Amount per serving (3 total)

Timing Information:

Preparation	10 m
Cooking	6 h
Total Time	6 h 20 m

Nutritional Information:

Calories	698 kcal
Fat	56.5 g
Carbohydrates	0g
Protein	44.1 g
Cholesterol	163 mg
Sodium	3647 mg

* Percent Daily Values are based on a 2,000 calorie diet.

FEIJOADA II

(BEAN STEW)

Ingredients

- 1 lb dry black beans
- 2 quarts water, plus more as needed
- 3 oz. dried beef, diced
- 1 bay leaf
- 2 smoked pork chops, cut into large chunks, bones reserved
- 4 oz. bacon, coarsely diced
- 12 oz. linguica sausage, cut into large chunks
- 2 (4 oz.) links Italian sausage
- 1 onion, diced
- 6 cloves garlic, minced
- 1 tsp ground cumin
- 1/2 tsp ground coriander
- 1 pinch cayenne pepper, or to taste
- salt and ground black pepper to taste

- 1 tbsp diced Italian parsley
- For the crumbs:
- 1 tbsp olive oil
- 1/2 C. dry bread crumbs
- 2 tbsps diced Italian parsley
- 2 tsps grated orange zest

Directions

- Let your beans sit in water for 8 hrs. Then rinse them and add them to a pot with 2 quarts of fresh water.
- Get the mix boiling, set the heat low, and cook everything for 90 mins.
- Now add the beef, beans, pork bones, and a bay leaf.
- Continue simmering the mix for 2 hrs.
- Now begin to stir fry your bacon until it is almost done and add the linguica and sausage.
- Stir fry this mix for 12 mins.

- Now dice your sausage into bite sized pieces when it is fully done and remove the bacon from the pan as well.
- Begin to stir fry your garlic and onions in the bacon drippings for 5 mins then add black pepper, cumin, salt, 1 tbsp parsley, coriander, and cayenne.
- Cook this mix for 3 more mins.
- Add the onions to the beans as well as: pork chop chunks, bacon, Italian sausage, and linguica.
- Turn up the heat and get everything gently boiling.
- Once it is boiling set the heat to a low level and cook the mix for 65 mins.
- Now toast your bread crumbs in olive oil for a few mins then add in 2 tbsp of parsley and orange zest.
- Garnish your beans with the bread crumb mix when serving.
- Enjoy.

Amount per serving (6 total)

Timing Information:

Preparation	30 m
Cooking	4 h 45 m
Total Time	13 h 15 m

Nutritional Information:

Calories	720 kcal
Fat	36.2 g
Carbohydrates	53.6g
Protein	45 g
Cholesterol	89 mg
Sodium	1625 mg

* Percent Daily Values are based on a 2,000 calorie diet.

WESTERN EUROPEAN GAZPACHO

Ingredients

- 3/4 green bell pepper, seeded
- 1/2 cucumber, peeled and sliced
- 2 cloves garlic, diced
- 1/2 C. olive oil
- 2 day-old crusty bread rolls, cut into thick slices
- 6 tomatoes, peeled and quartered
- 1/2 tbsp kosher salt
- 1 pinch cayenne pepper
- 1/2 tsp balsamic vinegar
- 1/4 tsp olive oil

Directions

- Process the following with a food processor: half C. olive oil, bell pepper, garlic, and cucumber.
- Add in your pieces of bread one by one then blend them.

- Place the mix in a bowl and add cayenne and salt.
- Place a covering of plastic around the bowl and put everything in the fridge for 65 mins.
- Top the dish with balsamic and 1/4 tsp of olive oil.
- Enjoy.

Amount per serving (4 total)

Timing Information:

Preparation	
Cooking	20 m
Total Time	1 h 20 m

Nutritional Information:

Calories	329 kcal
Fat	28.3 g
Carbohydrates	18.2g
Protein	3.5 g
Cholesterol	0 mg
Sodium	830 mg

* Percent Daily Values are based on a 2,000 calorie diet.

PORTUGUESE FRITTATA

Ingredients

- 16 eggs
- 1/4 C. milk
- 1 tbsp olive oil, or as needed
- 6 1/4-inch thick slices Genoa salami
- 1 C. diced fresh parsley, or more to taste
- 1/2 C. grated Parmesan cheese, divided
- 1/2 C. grated Romano cheese, divided
- 1/2 C. shredded mozzarella cheese, divided
- salt and ground black pepper to taste
- 1 pinch red pepper flakes, or to taste (optional)

Directions

- Set your oven to 425 degrees before doing anything else.
- Get a bowl, beat: milk and eggs.
- Get some olive oil hot then add in half of the egg mix.
- Place the salami on top of the egg and then add some parsley and 2/3 of the following: mozzarella, parmesan, and Romano.
- Add some pepper flakes, black pepper, and salt as well.
- Fry everything for 12 mins then add the rest of the egg and the rest of the cheeses.
- Add more pepper flakes, black pepper, and salt.
- Cook the frittata in the oven for 27 mins then serve the dish after letting it sit for 10 mins.
- Enjoy.

Amount per serving (8 total)

Timing Information:

Preparation	15 m
Cooking	30 m
Total Time	1 h 45 m

Nutritional Information:

Calories	262 kcal
Fat	18.7 g
Carbohydrates	2.6g
Protein	< 20.8 g
Cholesterol	397 mg
Sodium	1508 mg

* Percent Daily Values are based on a 2,000 calorie diet.

SPANISH DESSERT

(FLAN)

Ingredients

- 1/2 C. white sugar
- 2 C. milk
- 2 eggs, beaten
- 2 egg yolks, beaten
- 3/8 C. white sugar

Directions

- Set your oven to 350 degrees before doing anything else.
- Heat half a C. of sugar in a big pot until melted and golden.
- Then add the mix to some ramekins.
- Get another pan and get your milk almost boiling.

- Once the milk is hot add it gradually into whisked eggs and yolks.
- Add the sugar and then add everything to the ramekins.
- Place a wet towel into a roasting pan then put the ramekins on top.
- Now add some boiling water into the pan.
- Cook the ramekins in the oven for 45 mins.
- Then once the ramekins are no longer hot invert them in a baking dish.
- Enjoy.

Amount per serving (4 total)

Timing Information:

Preparation	10 m
Cooking	1 h
Total Time	1 h 10 m

Nutritional Information:

Calories	292 kcal
Fat	7.1 g
Carbohydrates	49.9g
Protein	8.5 g
Cholesterol	205 mg
Sodium	89 mg

* Percent Daily Values are based on a 2,000 calorie diet.

TUNA MOUSSE

Ingredients

- 15 pimento-stuffed green olives
- 1 (.25 oz.) package unflavored Jell-O(R)
- 2 (12.5 oz.) cans water-packed tuna, drained
- 1 C. mayonnaise
- 1/2 C. ketchup
- 1/4 tsp paprika
- 1 pinch white pepper
- 1 tbsp white sugar

Directions

- Slice your olives into 4 pieces with a crisscross pattern.
- Now coat a casserole dish with nonstick spray and layer your olives at the bottom.
- Begin to heat half a C. of water then add the gelatin, and

continue heating, while mixing, until everything is smooth.

- Blend the following with the blender: sugar, tuna, white pepper, mayo, paprika, and ketchup.
- Then add in the gelatin and continue processing.
- Layer this mix over the olives in the dish then place the mix in the fridge for 3 hrs.
- Enjoy.

Amount per serving (8 total)

Timing Information:

Preparation	
Cooking	20 m
Total Time	2 h 25 m

Nutritional Information:

Calories	321 kcal
Fat	23.4 g
Carbohydrates	7.3g
Protein	20.8 g
Cholesterol	34 mg
Sodium	747 mg

* Percent Daily Values are based on a 2,000 calorie diet.

LIVER AND ONIONS PORTUGUESE STYLE

Ingredients

- 2 onions, diced
- 1 tbsp olive oil
- 1 tsp dried thyme
- 1 tsp dried basil
- 1 tsp dried parsley
- salt and pepper to taste
- 1 C. sherry
- 1 lb calves' livers
- 1 tbsp diced fresh parsley
- 4 thick slices French bread, cut into 1 inch cubes
- 1/8 C. olive oil

Directions

- Coat your pieces of bread with olive oil then toast them in a pan until seared all over.

- Stir fry your onions until see through, in oil, then add in: pepper, thyme, salt, basil, and parsley.
- Stir the contents and add the sherry.
- Now get everything simmering.
- At the same time dice your liver then combine it with the sherry mix.
- Cook the contents for 8 mins then add some more sherry if needed.
- Top the mix with parsley and croutons.
- Enjoy.

Amount per serving (4 total)

Timing Information:

Preparation	10 m
Cooking	20 m
Total Time	30 m

Nutritional Information:

Calories	425 kcal
Fat	15 g
Carbohydrates	39.1g
Protein	28 g
Cholesterol	312 mg
Sodium	1668 mg

* Percent Daily Values are based on a 2,000 calorie diet.

POLLO AL AJILLO

(GARLIC AND CHICKEN STIR FRY)

Ingredients

- 1/4 C. extra virgin olive oil
- 1 (3 lb) whole chicken, cut into pieces
- 1 lb potatoes, peeled and cut into large chunks
- 18 cloves garlic, peeled
- 1 tsp freshly ground black pepper
- 3/4 tsp salt
- 2 tbsps diced fresh parsley
- 1 1/2 C. dry sherry
- 1/2 C. port wine

Directions

- Stir fry your chicken, in oil, with a lid on the pot until browned.

- Then place the chicken to the side.
- Add the potatoes to the same pot and layer your garlic on top of the potatoes.
- Add the chicken on top of everything then add parsley, salt, and pepper.
- Cover everything in sherry then place a lid on the pan.
- Cook the contents with a gentle boil for 50 mins.
- Enjoy.

Amount per serving (4 total)

Timing Information:

Preparation	30 m
Cooking	1 h
Total Time	1 h 30 m

Nutritional Information:

Calories	1077 kcal
Fat	65.5 g
Carbohydrates	139.5g
Protein	66.6 g
Cholesterol	1255 mg
Sodium	1224 mg

* Percent Daily Values are based on a 2,000 calorie diet.

PIPIRRANA

(POTATO SALAD FROM SPAIN)

Ingredients

- 6 eggs
- 6 potatoes, peeled and cubed
- 1 green bell pepper, seeded and diced
- 1 red bell pepper, seeded and diced
- 1/2 onion, diced
- 1 large fresh tomato, diced
- 1 (6 oz.) can tuna, drained
- 1/2 C. green olives with pimento or anchovy, halved
- 1/4 C. extra virgin olive oil
- 2 tbsps distilled white vinegar
- 1 tsp salt, or to taste

Directions

- Bring your water and eggs to a boil then place a lid on the pot and shut the heat.
- Let the eggs sit for 15 mins in the water.
- Now when the eggs are cool take off the shells and cut them into quarters.
- At the same time boil your potatoes in water and salt for 17 mins. Then place them in a bowl.
- Combine the following with the potatoes: vinegar, eggs, olive oil, bell peppers, green olives, onions, tuna, and tomatoes.
- Add in some pepper and salt. Then place the contents in the fridge until chilled.
- Enjoy.

Amount per serving (6 total)

Timing Information:

Preparation	30
Cooking	20 m
Total Time	2 h 50 m

Nutritional Information:

Calories	385 kcal
Fat	16.4 g
Carbohydrates	41.9g
Protein	18.6 g
Cholesterol	194 mg
Sodium	768 mg

* Percent Daily Values are based on a 2,000 calorie diet.

MAGGIE'S PORTUGUESE PAELLA

Ingredients

- 2 tbsps olive oil
- 1 tbsp paprika
- 2 tsps dried oregano
- salt and black pepper to taste
- 2 lbs skinless, boneless chicken breasts, cut into 2 inch pieces
- 2 tbsps olive oil, divided
- 3 cloves garlic, crushed
- 1 tsp crushed red pepper flakes
- 2 C. uncooked short-grain white rice
- 1 pinch saffron threads
- 1 bay leaf
- 1/2 bunch Italian flat leaf parsley, diced
- 1 quart chicken stock
- 2 lemons, zested
- 2 tbsps olive oil
- 1 Spanish onion, diced
- 1 red bell pepper, coarsely diced

- 1 lb chorizo sausage, casings removed and crumbled
- 1 lb shrimp, peeled and deveined

Directions

- Get a bowl, combine: pepper, 2 tbsps of olive oil, salt, oregano, and paprika.
- Add in the chicken and stir the contents.
- Place a covering of plastic around the bowl and put everything in the fridge.
- Now begin to stir fry your rice, pepper flakes, and garlic in 2 tbsps of olive oil for 5 mins.
- Then add in the lemon zest, saffron, stock, parsley, and bay leaf.
- Get everything boiling, then place a lid on the pot, and set the heat to low.
- Cook this mix for 23 mins.

- At the same time begin heating 2 tbsps of olive, the onions, and the chicken for 7 mins.
- Then add the shrimp and continue cooking until it is done.
- Layer your rice in a casserole dish and then layer the shrimp mix over everything.
- Enjoy.

Amount per serving (8 total)

Timing Information:

Preparation	30 m
Cooking	30 m
Total Time	1 h

Nutritional Information:

Calories	736 kcal
Fat	35.1 g
Carbohydrates	45.7g
Protein	55.7 g
Cholesterol	1202 mg
Sodium	1204 mg

* Percent Daily Values are based on a 2,000 calorie diet.

BACALAO A LA VIZCAINA

(CODFISH SOUP)

Ingredients

- 1 lb salted cod fish, soaked in water for 8 hours, refresh the water at least 3 times
- 4 potatoes, sliced thick
- 2 onions, sliced
- 4 hard-boiled eggs, sliced
- 2 tsps capers
- 2 large cloves garlic, minced
- 1/4 C. pitted green olives
- 1 (4 oz.) jar roasted red bell peppers, drained
- 1/2 C. golden raisins
- 1 bay leaf
- 1 (8 oz.) can tomato sauce
- 1/2 C. extra virgin olive oil
- 1 C. water
- 1/4 C. white wine

Directions

- Slice your fish into pieces.
- Now add the following to a Dutch oven in layers: potatoes, raisins, cod fish, roasted peppers, onions, olives, hard boiled eggs, garlic, and capers.
- Add a bay leaf, half of the olive oil, and half of the tomato sauce.
- Layer the rest of the ingredients in the same manner. Then add the water and wine.
- Place a lid on the pot and get everything boiling.
- Now set the heat to low and cook the mix for 35 mins.
- Enjoy.

Amount per serving (8 total)

Timing Information:

Preparation	30 m
Cooking	45 m
Total Time	9 h 15 m

Nutritional Information:

Calories	475 kcal
Fat	18.9 g
Carbohydrates	31.6g
Protein	42.3 g
Cholesterol	192 mg
Sodium	4353 mg

* Percent Daily Values are based on a 2,000 calorie diet.

ESPETADAS

(BEEF KABOBS)

Ingredients

- 3/4 C. red wine
- 8 cloves garlic
- 6 bay leaves, crumbled
- 2 tbsps coarse salt
- freshly ground pepper to taste
- 3 lbs beef sirloin steak, cut into cubes
- bamboo skewers, soaked in water for 60 minutes

Directions

- Get a bowl, combine: black pepper, wine, salt, bay leaves, and garlic.
- Combine in the beef then stir the mix.

- Place a covering on the bowl and put everything in the fridge for 8 hrs.
- Get your grill hot and oil the grate.
- Now grill your beef after placing them on skewers.
- Cook the kabobs on the grill for about 5 mins per side.
- Enjoy.

Amount per serving (10 total)

Timing Information:

Preparation	10 m
Cooking	10 m
Total Time	8 h 20 m

Nutritional Information:

Calories	190 kcal
Fat	7.8 g
Carbohydrates	1.4g
Protein	< 23.8 g
Cholesterol	59 mg
Sodium	1446 mg

* Percent Daily Values are based on a 2,000 calorie diet.

THANKS FOR READING! NOW LET'S TRY SOME SUSHI AND DUMP DINNERS....

Send the Book!

To grab this **box set** simply follow the link mentioned above, or tap the book cover.

This will take you to a page where you can simply enter your email address and a PDF version of the **box set** will be emailed to you.

I hope you are ready for some serious cooking!

Send the Book!

You will also receive updates about all my new books when they are free.

Also don't forget to like and subscribe on the social networks. I love meeting my readers. Links to all my profiles are below so please click and connect :)

Facebook

Twitter

Come On...
Let's Be Friends :)

I adore my readers and love connecting with them socially. Please follow the links below so we can connect on Facebook, Twitter, and Google+.

Facebook

Twitter

I also have a blog that I regularly update for my readers so check it out below.

My Blog

CAN I ASK A FAVOUR?

If you found this book interesting, or have otherwise found any benefit in it. Then may I ask that you post a review of it on Amazon? Nothing excites me more than new reviews, especially reviews which suggest new topics for writing. I do read all reviews and I always factor feedback into my newer works.

So if you are willing to take ten minutes to write what you sincerely thought about this book then please visit our Amazon page and post your opinions.

Again thank you!

INTERESTED IN OTHER EASY COOKBOOKS?

Everything is easy! Check out my Amazon Author page for more great cookbooks:

For a complete listing of all my books please see my author page.

22872458R00095

Printed in Great Britain
by Amazon